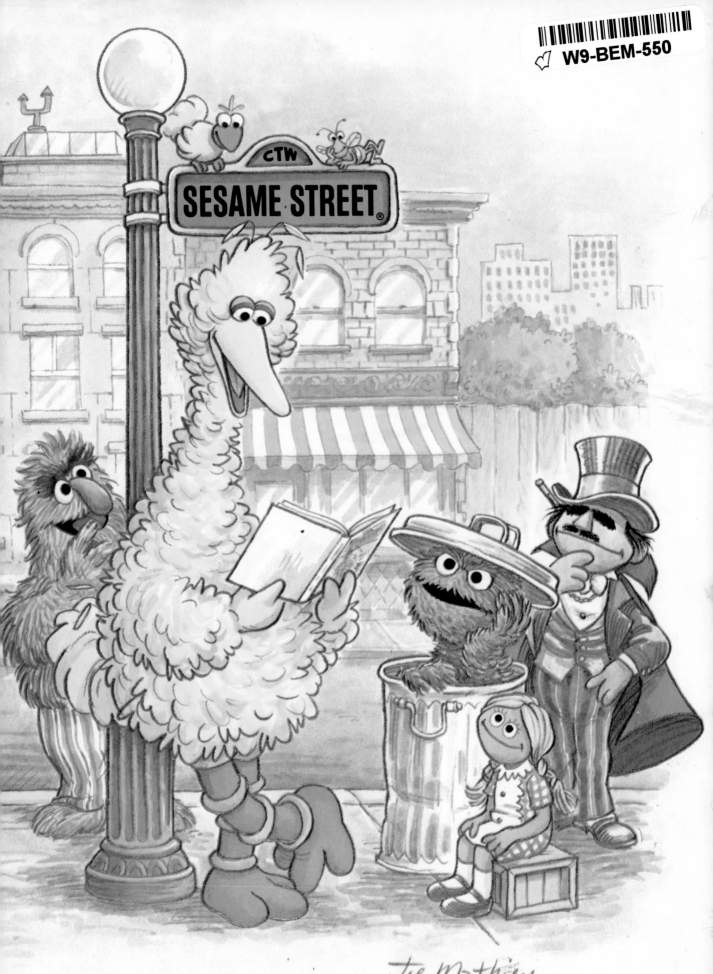

THE
SESAME STREET®
LIBRARY

With Jim Henson's Muppets

VOLUME 13

FEATURING
THE NUMBER
13

Children's Television Workshop/Funk & Wagnalls, Inc.

WRITTEN BY:
Emily Perl Kingsley
Patricia Thackray

ILLUSTRATED BY:
Bill Basso
Richard Brown
Ivan Chermayeff
Tom Cooke
Robert Dennis
Lawrence Di Fiori
Thomas Herbert
Ruth Marten
Joseph Mathieu
Marc Nadel
Gary Schenck
Michael J. Smollin

PHOTOGRAPHS BY:
Richard Hutchings
Douglas Kelley

BERT AND ERNIE AND THE GREAT RACE

Featuring the Number 13

Oh, no, Ernie! We got number 13! We'll never win this race!!

Why not, old buddy?

Ready! Set!! GO!!!

The number thirteen is BAD LUCK!!

Don't be silly, Bert. This is my lucky day!

Never go under a ladder, Ernie! It's BAD LUCK!!

Relax, Bert. That's just superstition.

ROUTE 13

Hey, it's Biff and Sully. Wave to them, Bert!

I can't look!

13

The grass is greener over there!

Right, Elma! Let's jump over!

Ernie, watch out for jumping sheep!

What sheep, Bert!?

Stop, Ernie! A black cat!! If it crosses our path, we'll lose the race!

BAAAA!!!!

Don't bother me, Bert. I have to keep my eyes on the road!

It's Sherlock Hemlock!

The Case of the Missing Hat

I'm looking up! I'm looking down!
I'm looking for the color **brown**!

I'm looking for it everywhere!
Ah-ha! I see a big **brown** bear!

A big **brown** bear with big **brown** shoes . . .
Uh-oh! I think he's got the blues.

Excuse me, Bear, but why the tears?
The big **brown** bear cries, "It's my ears!"

"They're cold without my big **brown** hat—
I lost it (sniff) and that is that."

Oh, don't be sad—for help is here!
We'll find your big **brown** hat—don't fear.

We're looking up! We're looking down!
We're looking for a hat that's **brown**!

Can you find the **brown** hat in the picture?
Circle the **brown** hat.

The Count's Counting Page

Greetings, my friends! It is I, the Count!
The numbers 1 to 13 are hidden somewhere on this page.
I want to count them, but I can't find them.
Can you help me?
Circle the numbers, 1 to 13.
Now, count the numbers 1 to 13.

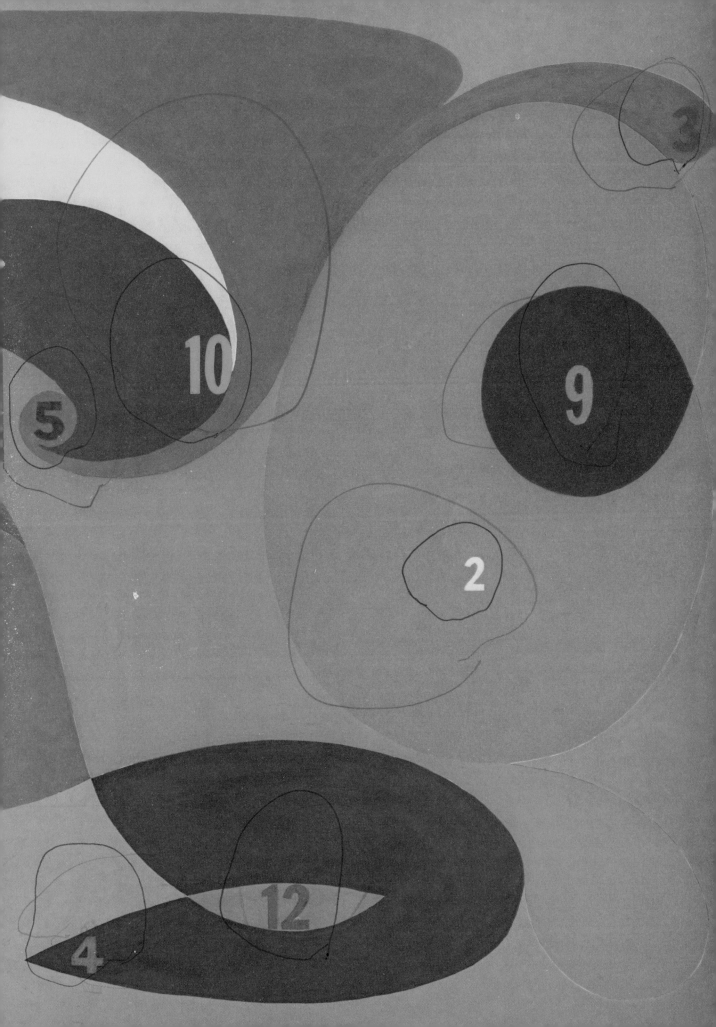

With Love from Me to Me

Hello, everybody! Let us play a little word game. Here is a picture of me, cute little Grover. Do you see the lines pointing to parts of my furry body? You do? Oh, good. Near each line is a word. Do you know what the words say? Guess. The word that is matched to my leg says ___. Yes! That is right! It says LEG. Guess what the other words say.

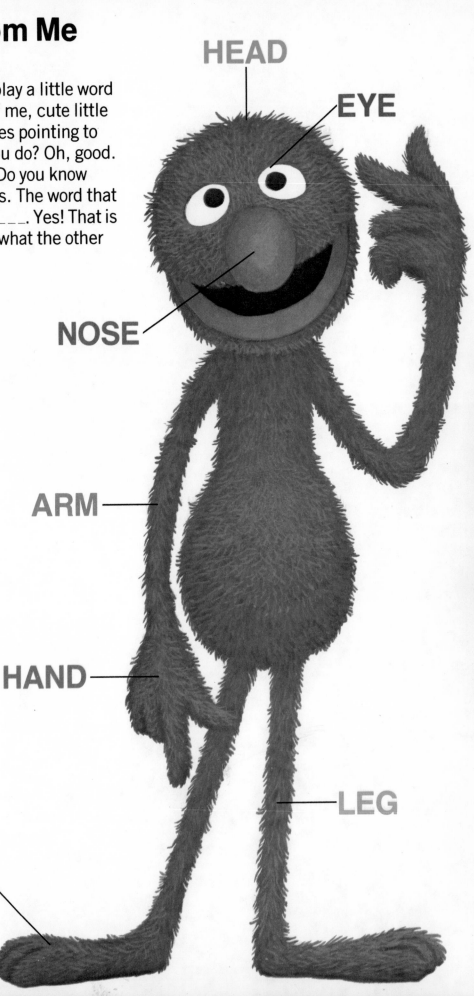

HEAD

EYE

NOSE

ARM

HAND

LEG

FOOT

Now I will tell you a story. All those nice words are in this story. Will you help me? See if you can tell what all the words in pretty colors say. Here we go!

Foot, I like you, Foot.

One day, I said FOOT, I like you, FOOT. You can hop. LEG, I said, I like you, LEG. You are a friend of FOOT. HAND, I said, I like you. You are fun. ARM, I said, you are wonderful, ARM. You can lift my HAND way up. EYE, I said, I am so proud that you can see things. NOSE, I said, I love you, NOSE. You are so cute. HEAD, I said, Grover likes you very much. You are always thinking.
So, I made my FOOT, LEG, HAND, ARM, EYE, NOSE and HEAD feel very good that day. The end.

The sky's the limit!
All the things on this page begin with the letter S.
Can you name the S-words?

Sky

Super Grover

Satellite

Santa in a Sled

Spaceship

Star

Sun

Cookie's Cooking!

Cookie is making some yummy peanut butter balls for a party!
You can make them too!
You *measure* things to see how much you have.
You will need to *measure* the things that go into your peanut butter balls.
You use a *cup* and a *teaspoon* to measure.

This is a teaspoon.

This is a cup.

Mix until smooth.

Put 2 cups **peanut butter**, 2 cups
honey and 2 teaspoons **powdered
milk** into a bowl.

Add 1 teaspoon **oats** and 2 teaspoons
mixed raisins and nuts.

Mix again until
evenly blended.

Roll this mixture into small
balls with your hands.

Place the balls on
the cookie sheet.

Put the cookie sheet in the refrigerator.

Let the balls sit in the refrigerator
for about 4 hours.

Ernie's Balloons

Ernie was walking down Sesame Street holding a string that had a big red balloon tied to it. The balloon was floating way up over Ernie's head.

"Wow, what a great balloon this is," said Ernie. "This is the best balloon I've ever had!"

Then Ernie walked by a tree, and his balloon got stuck in some branches. When he tried to pull it out, it popped!

"Oh, no!" cried Ernie. "My balloon popped. My favorite balloon …gee, that makes me sad." Ernie started to cry. "Ohhh, my best balloon popped, and I bet nobody cares. Everybody's off playing somewhere, and they don't care that my balloon popped and that I'm sad."

As Ernie cried, Maria came up to him with a big blue balloon. Maria said, "I saw your balloon pop, Ernie, and I know you're sad, so I got you another one to cheer you up. Here you go." Maria gave the balloon to Ernie and walked away.

"Uh, gee, thanks, Maria," said Ernie. "Somebody does care."

Then Cookie Monster came up to Ernie with a bright green balloon. "Ernie," said Cookie, "me heard your balloon popped and you sad. Me don't like to see you sad, so here." And Cookie Monster gave the balloon to Ernie and walked away.

Ernie said, cheering up, "You got me a balloon too, Cookie Monster? Oh, boy!"

Then Big Bird came up to Ernie with a big pink balloon. "Hi, Ernie," said Big Bird. "I heard that your balloon popped and that you were sad. So I got this special balloon just for you."

"Gee, thanks, Big Bird," said Ernie.

"Hey, Ernie baby!" said Grover, running up to Ernie. "I heard your balloon popped. Here is a pretty yellow balloon from your friend, Grover."

"And here's an orange one from your buddy Bert," said Bert.

Before Ernie could say thank you to Grover and Bert, the Count came up to him with eight red balloons. "Hello, Ernie, my friend," said the Count. "I heard that your one balloon popped, so I brought you eight wonderful, red balloons. Count them and you will feel much better!"

Everybody on Sesame Street brought Ernie a balloon because no one wanted him to be sad. Ernie had lots of balloons floating over his head. He said, "Look at all these balloons! Gee, everybody does care, and that sure does make me happy!"

What is a blimp?

Look! Look high up in the sky! There's something flying above us. What is it? It's a blimp! What is a blimp? A blimp is like an airplane. An airplane flies—so does a blimp. A blimp is like a balloon. A balloon has air in it—so does a blimp. A blimp is like a flying balloon! What lifts a blimp up? Gas lifts the blimp up. The gas that lifts the blimp up is called **helium**. The helium is kept in the huge body of the blimp. What makes the blimp go? An engine and a propeller make the blimp go. A blimp can carry all sorts of things. The people ride in a little room underneath the blimp's body. There are not many blimps anymore. Someday, you might see one!

13!

Presents! Wonderful, wonderful presents!
I love to count presents! Count all the
presents! How many are there? Whom do
you think the presents are for?

basso

Betty Lou Lends a Hand

"My, what a blustery, blowy day," said Bert as he stepped out onto Sesame Street. "This is the strongest wind we've had around here in a long time."

Bert held his coat tightly closed against the wind and noticed that all of his friends were out playing touch football in the yard.

"Hey, everybody," called Bert, holding up a small white envelope in his hand. "Come here! I have something to show you!"

Bert's friends stopped their game of touch football and came over to Bert.

"What is it?" asked Ernie.

"Yeah, what've you got there that's so wonderful?" asked Roosevelt Franklin.

"I bet it's a new paper clip for his paper clip collection," Farley whispered to Grover.

"... Or some new pictures of pigeons or something boring like that."

"Oh, it's so fantastic," said Bert, "I can't wait to show you!"

"So let's see it!" said Prairie Dawn. "We interrupted our game of touch football to come over here and see what it is."

Just as Bert was about to open the envelope and show everybody what was in it, a big gust of wind whipped the envelope out of his hand and blew it up into the air.

"Oh, no!" cried Bert. "My

a lot of friends here. I'm sure someone will be able to get the envelope out of there for you."

"Sure, Bert," said Herry. "I'm the *strongest* person here so I'm sure I can get your envelope back for you. And even if there is only a silly, dumb picture of a pigeon inside, I'll help you get it back.

"Now stand back, everybody, and make way for the *strongest* one of all. I will just lift that fence up into

envelope!! The wind is blowing it away! Help!"

The wind carried the envelope high in the air, twisting and turning it, dipping and darting it, sailing it over a big wooden construction fence and onto the ground on the other side.

"Oh, gosh," wailed Bert. "My envelope's behind that big fence. Now what am I going to do?!"

"Gee, Bert," said Ernie. "You have

the air so you can go underneath and grab your envelope. I bet you're glad *I* am here today! Ya!"

Herry grabbed a corner of the fence and pulled up with all his might, but the fence was very firmly planted and he couldn't lift it out of the ground.

"Gee, Herry, thanks a lot," said Bert. "You are very strong, but it looks like strength isn't what we need to get my envelope back."

"Let me try," said Big Bird. "I'm the *biggest*. I'll just reach right over the top of the fence and get your envelope for you. Even if it is just a silly old picture of a pigeon, it's important to you, so I'll help you get it back. Now everybody watch closely as the biggest one here gets the envelope. Here goes...."

Big Bird stood up on tippy-toes and reached as far as he could over the top of the wooden fence, but the fence was too high. Big Bird couldn't reach far enough to get the envelope.

"I'm sorry, Bert," said Big Bird. "I guess bigness is not what you need, either."

"What you need is *smartness*," said Sherlock Hemlock, "and I am the world's smartest detective. I will get that envelope out of there."

"Ahhh," said Bert. "Smartness. Now that's a good idea."

Sherlock Hemlock went over to a skinny little crack in the fence and put his mouth up against it.

"Now, little white envelope on the ground in there, I, Sherlock Hemlock, the world's smartest detective, am talking to you," he said through the crack. "I think you ought to realize how upset you have made our friend Bert by flying over that fence. And even though you probably have nothing but a silly, boring old picture of a pigeon inside you, I think that the *sensible* thing would be for you to come out of there and stop causing Bert so much distress. Now, what do you say?"

Naturally, the envelope just lay there on the ground. Sherlock

Hemlock threw up his hands. "This
silly envelope is *not* responding
to logic and reason. I do not
understand it."

Bert sighed. "I guess it has no
respect for smartness."

"May *I* help?" asked the Count.

"Sure," said Bert. "What do *you*
think?"

"I think that you have had three
suggestions that did not work.
Three! You had the strongest, the
biggest, and the smartest. That
makes three no-good suggestions!
Ah-hahahahaha! Happy to be able
to help, Bert."

"That didn't help!" snapped Bert.

"Say, Bert," said the Cookie
Monster. "Me the *hungriest*. How
about this? Me eat this fence up.
Then you can go get envelope. Me
not do that for silly, boring picture
of pigeon. Me do that because me so
hungry and fence look pretty good."

"Oh, Cookie Monster," moaned
Bert. "I'm ready to try anything.
Eating a fence sounds crazy to me,
but if you feel up to it . . ."

Cookie Monster went over to the
fence and took a great big, huge
bite out of it.

"Blecchhh!" he cried. "That the
most terrible fence me ever eat!
Boy! Need salt! Need ketchup! Need
Worcestershire sauce! No way me
can eat whole fence that taste like
that! Sorry, Bert. Me want to help
but there a limit even to what *me*
can eat!"

"*Four* terrible, awful, silly, no-
good ideas!" yelled the Count.

"How about *me*?" called Rodeo
Rosie. "I'm the *loudest*! You just give

me a crack at it and I'll have your silly old pigeon picture back in two shakes!"

"Go ahead, Rodeo Rosie," shrugged Bert.

Rodeo Rosie sauntered up to the fence and put her hands up to her mouth.

"NOW LISTEN HERE, ENVELOPE! YOU GIT ON OUTA THERE RIGHT PRONTO, Y'HEAR? I GIVE YA A COUNT OF THREE TO JIST SKEDADDLE RIGHT ON OUT HERE WHERE YA B'LONG!! A-ONE, A-TWO, A-THREE!!" she hollered.

"That certainly was loud," said Bert, rubbing his ears. "But the envelope's still sitting there, just like before. Thanks, Rodeo Rosie, but I guess loudness wasn't what we needed either."

Bert gave a deep sigh. "Say, how about *you*, Betty Lou?" he said. "You're the only one who hasn't made a suggestion. Don't you have

any ideas about how to get my
envelope back?"

"Me?" said Betty Lou. "Well, I am
not the biggest or the strongest or
the loudest or the smartest. All I am
is the *smallest*. What could I
possibly do for you?"

"I don't know," said Bert. "But the
biggest and the strongest and the
loudest and the smartest haven't

done much good. I thought you could
come up with something."

"Well, let me look," said Betty
Lou.

She walked up to the skinny little
crack in the fence and looked
through. There was the white
envelope, still lying on the ground.
Betty Lou was about to turn away
when she thought of something.

"Hey," she said. "I'm so small that if I held my hand all flat like this ... and held my arm out straight like this ... maybe, just maybe I could just squeeze my little arm right through that crack ... like this ... and reach your envelope with my fingers ... like THIS!!"

And she grabbed the envelope with her fingers and pulled it through the narrow crack in the fence. She held it up high for all to see.

"Hooray for Betty Lou!" everyone shouted.

"Wow," she said. "I did it! I didn't have to be the biggest or the strongest or the smartest or the loudest or anything!! In fact, being the *smallest* was just what you needed! How about that!"

"That's right, Betty Lou," said Bert. "Thank you!"

Bert smiled broadly. "Well, now

that we have the envelope back, wouldn't you all like to see what's in it?"

"Oh, we know what it is, Bert," said Ernie. "Just some silly, boring old picture of a pigeon for your scrapbook. We knew that all along. Probably just a silly old pigeon eating birdseed...."

"Or a pigeon walking on the ground," said Prairie Dawn.

"Or a pigeon sitting on a statue," suggested Herry.

"*I'd* like to see what's in the envelope, Bert," said Betty Lou. "Please?"

"Well, as a matter of fact," said Bert, "it just happens to be ... tickets to the circus for me ... and all my friends!"

"Tickets? For the circus? For your friends?" said Ernie, swallowing hard.

"For *all* your friends?" asked Big Bird. "Even the ones who kept teasing you about having a dumb old pigeon picture in there?"

"ALL my friends," shouted Bert, happily. "My strong friends ... and my big friends ... and my smart friends ... and my little friends ... and my fast friends ... and my slow friends ... for *all* my friends!"

"Yaaaay Bert!" cried all his friends.

And they all started out for the circus together.

"And on our way to the circus," said Bert, "I'll tell you all about the great pigeon act we're going to see there. This circus has the *best* trained pigeons! We'll actually see a pigeon stand on one foot. And then we'll see a pigeon who *sits down*. And after that, a pigeon eating a piece of bread.... And guess what comes after that?! ..."

How do birds learn to fly?

A bird learns how to fly when it is a baby—
just as you learned how to walk when you were
a baby.
The baby bird moves around a lot in its nest.
It wriggles and squirms and stretches and
twists. This is how it makes its wings strong.
When its wings are strong, the baby bird can
use them to fly.
When you were a baby, you wriggled and
squirmed and stretched and twisted. That is
how you made your legs strong. When your
legs were strong enough, you used them
to walk.
The mother bird teaches the baby how to fly.
She puts food in her mouth and goes a little
bit away from the nest. She knows the baby
bird wants the food. The baby bird must leave
the nest and fly to get to its mother and
the food.
A baby bird tries over and over again to fly.
Each time it flies, it gets better and better.
Soon it will fly as well as its mother. When you
were little, you tried over and over again to
walk. And now see what you can do!

The Juggler

Grover is a juggler in the circus.
He is juggling shapes.
1. Point to the **green** circle.
2. Find the **red** triangle.
3. What other shapes does Grover have?
What colors are they?

Look closely at Grover's shapes.
Try to remember them.
Now turn the page.

Which shapes are missing?

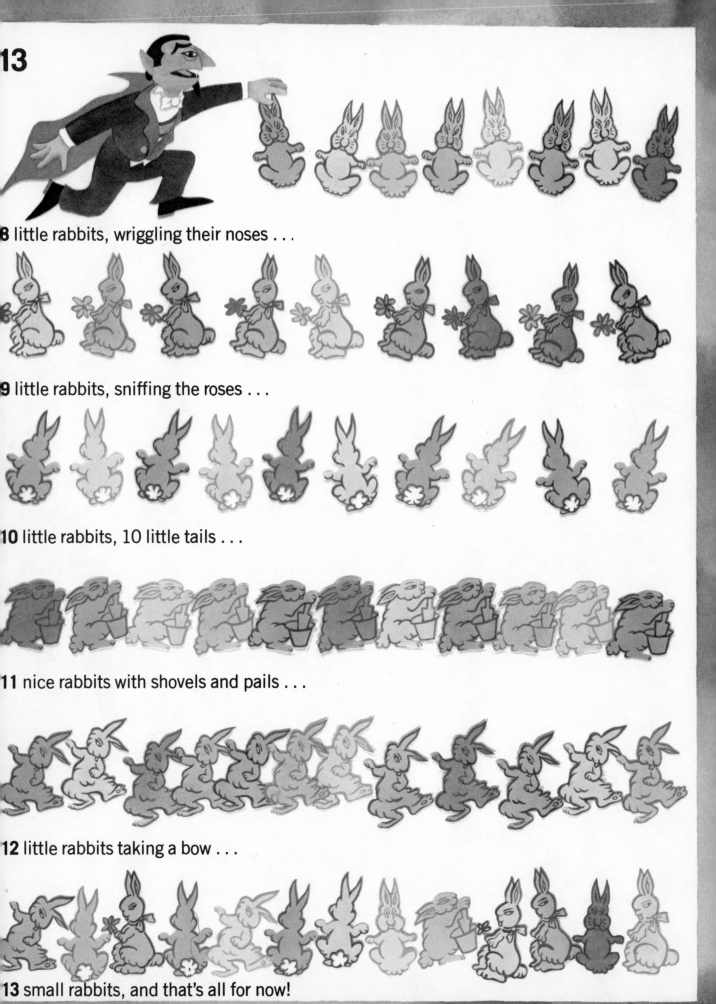

13

8 little rabbits, wriggling their noses . . .

9 little rabbits, sniffing the roses . . .

10 little rabbits, 10 little tails . . .

11 nice rabbits with shovels and pails . . .

12 little rabbits taking a bow . . .

13 small rabbits, and that's all for now!

Ruth Marten

START

START

START

It's Play-Day!

Three of your friends have been playing in the playground!
What have they been doing?

Follow the blue arrows to find out what Grover did.
Tell a story about Grover in the playground.

Follow the yellow arrows to find out what Big Bird did.
Tell a story about Big Bird in the playground.

Follow the green arrows to find out what Oscar the Grouch did.
Tell a story about Oscar the Grouch in the playground.

What are Grover, Big Bird and Oscar the Grouch doing now?

13

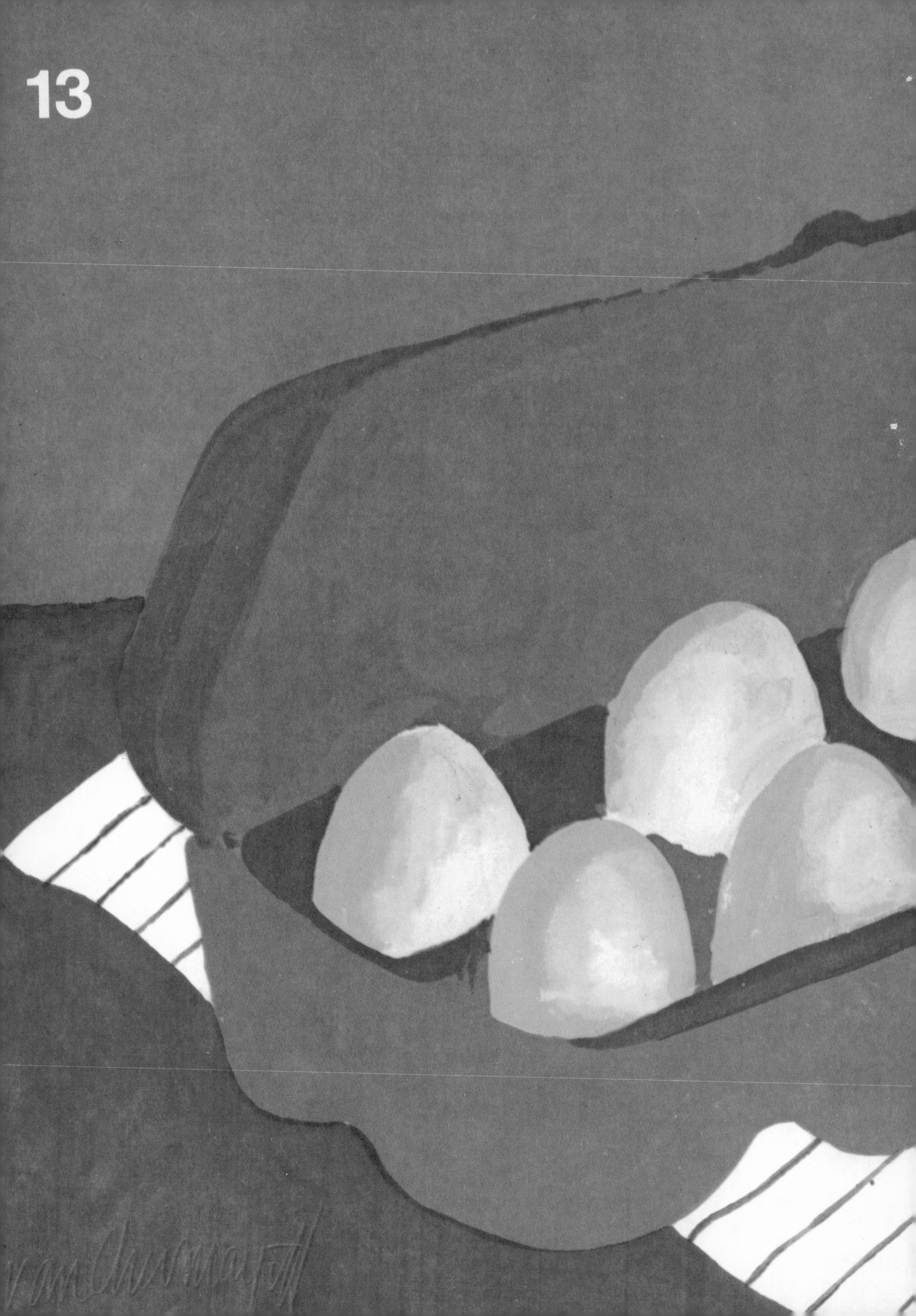

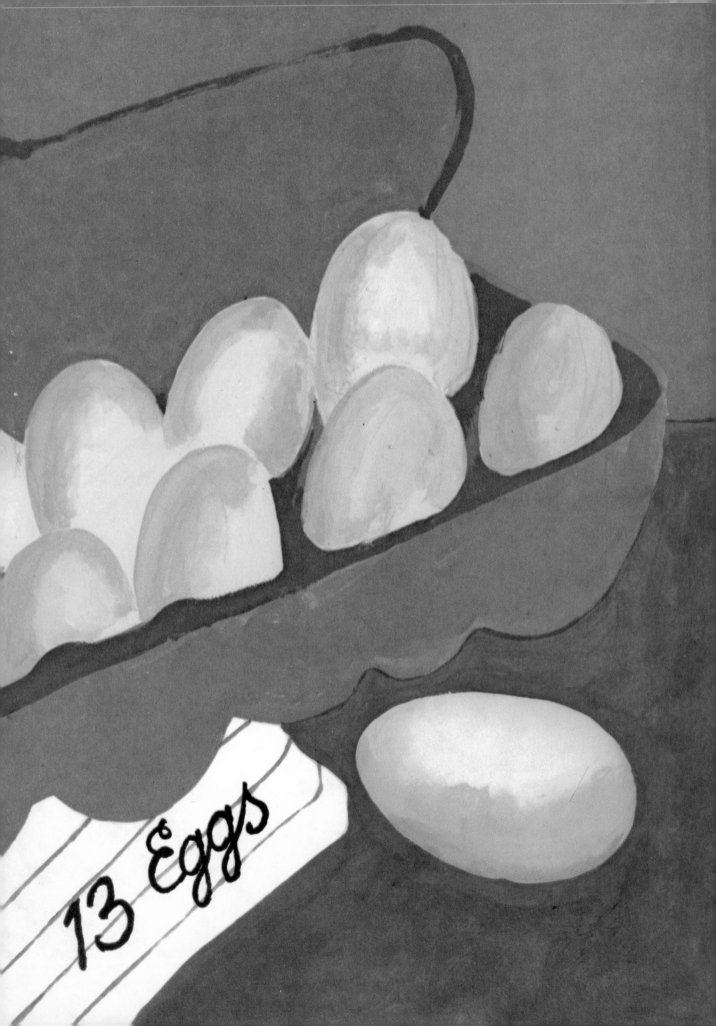

13 Eggs

Bedtime Story

Ernie and Bert were in their bedroom at Grandma Bottle's house. (Grandma Bottle is Bert's grandmother). They were making their beds. Ernie tucked his blanket under his bed and fluffed his pillow. Then he looked over at Bert's bed. He saw that Bert's bed was all wrinkled and messy.

"Hey, Bert, what's the matter?" asked Ernie.

"Gee, Ernie, old buddy, I just don't feel like making my bed. Besides, I'm not very good at it yet," said Bert.

"But Bert," said Ernie, "It's easy! You love being neat. I bet you can make a really neat bed. You just need practice."

"I just can't seem to do it right, Ernie," said Bert. "Do you think you could help me?"

"Sure, Bert," said Ernie. Ernie walked over to Bert's bed and started to straighten the covers.

"Wait a minute, Bert," said Ernie, "I have a great idea! Why don't you get *in* the bed? Then you can see exactly what I'm doing."

Bert scratched his head. "I don't think that will work, Ernie."

"Bert, old pal, it's worth a try."

Before Bert could answer, Ernie gently pushed him into his bed. Then Ernie started to show Bert how to make his bed. He explained very carefully what he was doing. First he straightened out the sheets under Bert. Then he pulled the blanket tightly across the bed and neatly tucked it in. Finally Ernie fluffed Bert's pillow and placed it gently under Bert's head.

"That's how you make a bed." Ernie said proudly. "Now isn't that fun Bert? Bert? Bert . . . ?"

Bert did not answer. He was fast asleep in his snugly bed.

"Have a nice nap, Bert," Ernie whispered. And he tiptoed out of the room.